CITIES THROUGH TIME

Beijing

by Kate Moening
Illustrated by Diego Vaisberg

BELLWETHER MEDIA
MINNEAPOLIS, MN

Blastoff! Missions takes you on a learning adventure! Colorful illustrations and exciting narratives highlight cool facts about our world and beyond. Read the mission goals and follow the narrative to gain knowledge, build reading skills, and have fun!

Traditional Nonfiction

Narrative Nonfiction

Blastoff! Universe

MISSION GOALS

- FIND YOUR SIGHT WORDS IN THE BOOK.
- LEARN ABOUT DIFFERENT PERIODS IN BEIJING'S HISTORY.
- LEARN ABOUT RULERS THAT HAVE SHAPED BEIJING.

This edition first published in 2025 by Bellwether Media, Inc.

Library of Congress Cataloging-in-Publication Data

LC record for Beijing available at: https://lccn.loc.gov/2024046814

Editor: Christina Leaf Designer: Laura Sowers

Printed in the United States of America, North Mankato, MN.

This is **Blastoff Jimmy**! He is here to help you on your mission and share fun facts along the way!

Table of Contents

Welcome to Beijing!

Beijing, China, is a busy place! More than 21 million people live in and around the city.

Beijing has been a capital city for centuries. Let's visit its past!

Age of Emperors

221 BCE

Shi Huangdi has destroyed the city of Ji. He has taken over the Yan kingdom.

He will be China's first **emperor**! He will join all of China's kingdoms together under his rule.

early 1200s CE

Genghis Khan attacks the city! His army sets the **palaces** on fire. They will burn for more than a month.

He wants to rule
all of China.
Genghis Khan

1420

The Ming **dynasty** rules the city! Workers are finishing the Forbidden City. This new palace has a golden roof.

JIMMY SAYS

Ji City had many names. The Ming named it Beijing! The name means "northern capital."

Outside the city, workers add to the Great Wall.

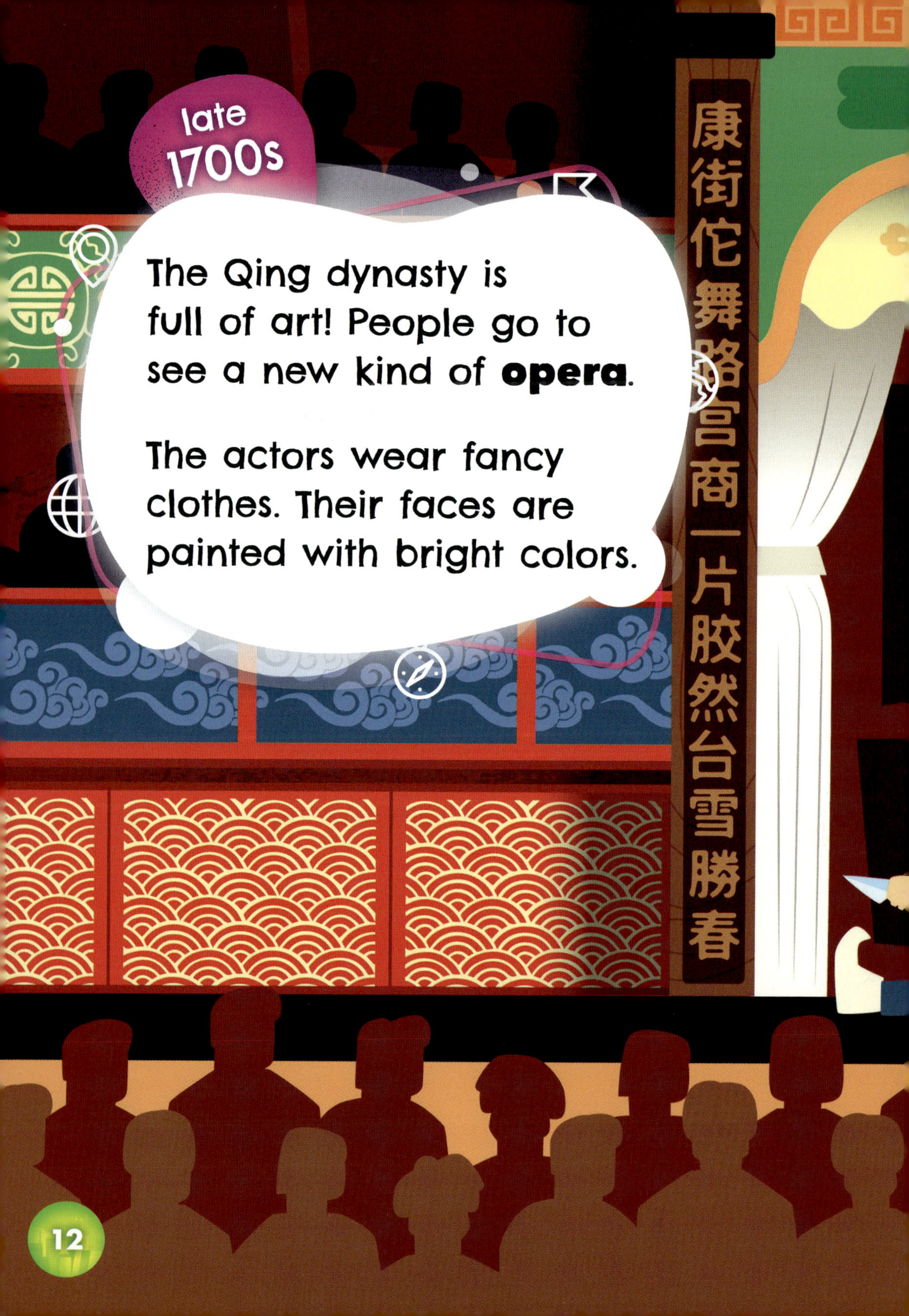

late 1700s

The Qing dynasty is full of art! People go to see a new kind of **opera**.

The actors wear fancy clothes. Their faces are painted with bright colors.

Beijing
opera

Changes in China

1900

Many outsiders now live in China. Some people want them to leave.

The Boxers attack Beijing. They burn the homes of outsiders. They burn churches, too. Their **siege** lasts for weeks.

1949

China's **civil war** is over. Mao Zedong gives a speech in Beijing.

He says China will be
a **communist** country.
He will lead with a harsh rule.

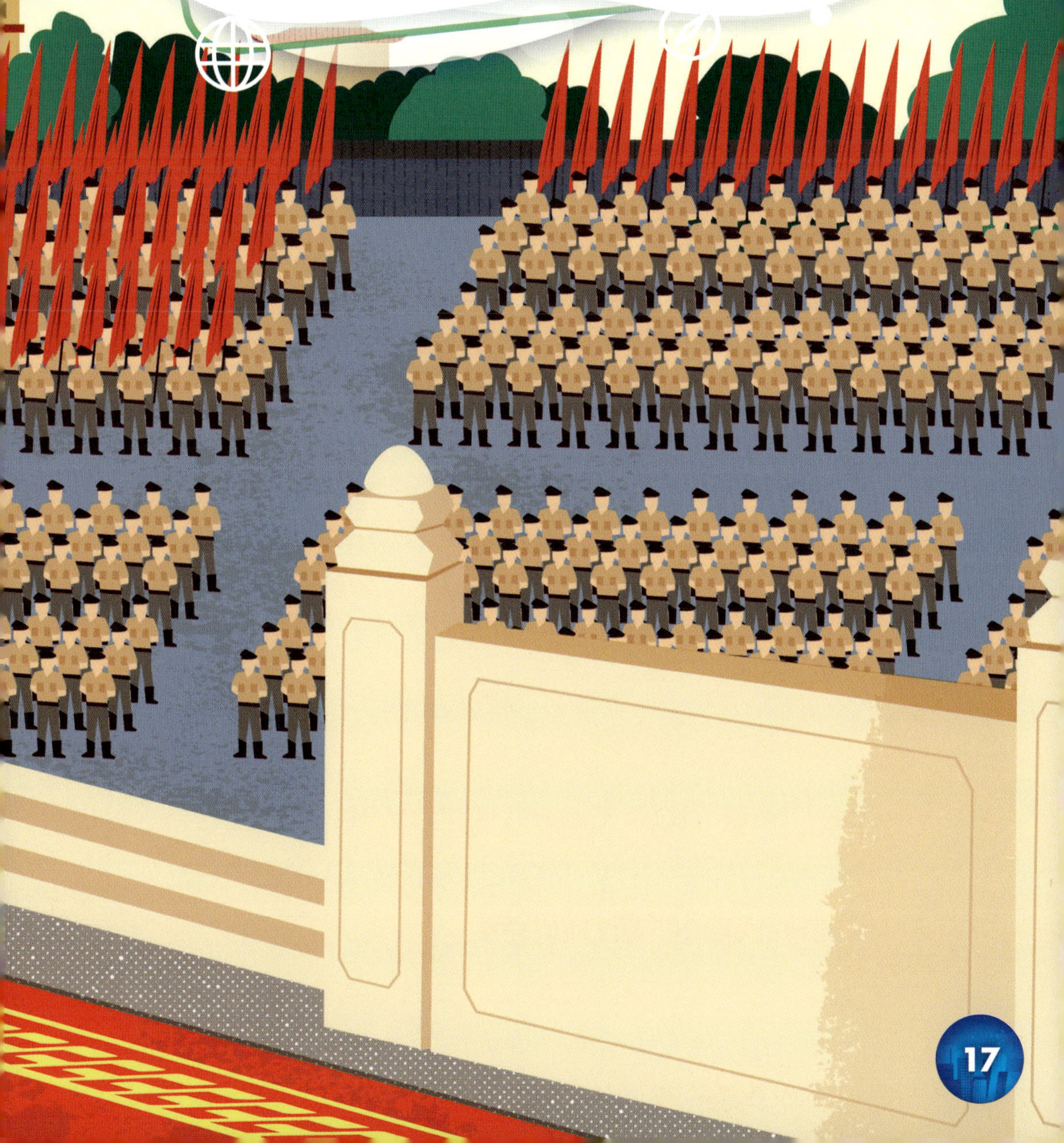

2008

Beijing has been growing fast! Now the city holds the Summer **Olympic Games**.

Drummers march in the Beijing National **Stadium**. Fireworks light up the night sky. The Games begin!

The City Today

today

Many **ancient** buildings still stand. People ride buses, trains, cars, and bikes. They do **tai chi** in parks. They gather in tea shops.

Beijing buzzes with history and modern life!

Beijing Timeline

221 BCE: Shi Huangdi destroys the city of Ji and takes over

early 1200s CE: Genghis Khan's army burns the city and takes over

1420: Workers finish building the Forbidden City

late 1700s: Beijing opera arises during the Qing dynasty

1900: People attack outsiders in Beijing in the Boxer Rebellion

1949: Mao Zedong makes China a communist country

2008: Beijing hosts the Summer Olympic Games

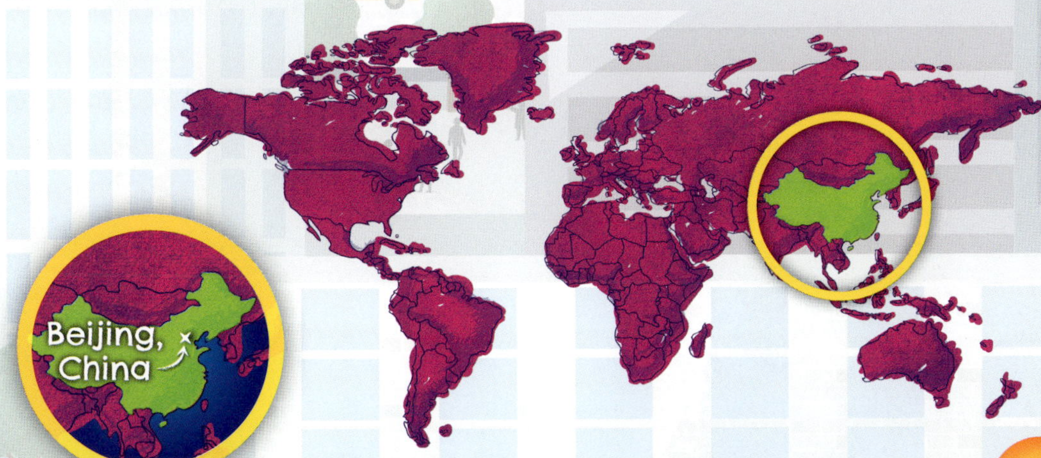

Glossary

ancient—very old

civil war—a war between groups of people in the same country

communist—related to a system where the government owns goods, services, and property

dynasty—a family of rulers who rule a country for a long time

emperor—the ruler of an empire

Olympic Games—worldwide summer or winter sports contests held in a different country every four years

opera—a kind of play in which actors sing all or most of the words

palaces—the official homes of emperors or other leaders

siege—an attack that continues for a long time

stadium—a very large building used for sports, events, and concerts

tai chi—a form of exercise that uses very slow movements

To Learn More

AT THE LIBRARY

Gould, Sloane, and Ruth Bjorklund. *China*. New York, N.Y.: Cavendish Square Publishing, 2023.

Lee, Jean Kuo. *Huangdi: Yellow Emperor*. Minneapolis, Minn.: Kids Core, 2023.

Mather, Charis. *A Visit to China*. Minneapolis, Minn.: Bearport, 2023.

ON THE WEB

FACTSURFER

Factsurfer.com gives you a safe, fun way to find more information.

1. Go to www.factsurfer.com.
2. Enter "Beijing" into the search box and click 🔍.
3. Select your book cover to see a list of related content.

BEYOND THE MISSION

> WHAT FACT FROM THE BOOK DID YOU THINK WAS THE MOST INTERESTING?

> WHY DO YOU THINK INVADERS BURNED BEIJING? HOW DID THIS HELP THEM GAIN POWER?

> DESIGN A COSTUME FOR THE BEIJING OPERA. DRAW A PICTURE.

Index